Think with the Heart
Love with the Mind

WORKBOOK

Copyright © 2017 Paul Dugliss / New World Ayurveda, LLC. All rights reserved.

Cover Image Credits:
Abstract Heart: Bobbie Sandlin @ 123RF.com
Beautiful Painting Goddess Woman with Ornamental Mandala: Jozef Klopacka @ 123RF.com
Telepathy: Andrea Danti @ 123RF.com

Dedication

Knowledge applied with love cultivates wisdom. That is the purpose of this workbook — to apply the knowledge of self-development to create lasting transformation and ultimate wisdom, liberation, bliss and love. I dedicate this book to the betterment of all humanity through the glorious achievements of your Divine Self. May it be so.

Introduction

Until one is committed, there is hesitancy, the chance to draw back — Concerning all acts of initiative (and creation), there is one elementary truth that ignorance of which kills countless ideas and splendid plans: that the moment one definitely commits oneself, then Providence moves too. All sorts of things occur to help one that would never otherwise have occurred. A whole stream of events issues from the decision, raising in one's favor all manner of unforeseen incidents and meetings and material assistance, which no man could have dreamed would have come his way. Whatever you can do, or dream you can do, begin it. Boldness has genius, power, and magic in it. Begin it now.

- Goethe

If you want to accelerate your inner growth and development, the most important thing you can do is to make the commitment to do so. Schedule time on your calendar each day for the next 30 days to do the exercises in this book. This is an important technique for making commitments. The exercises do not require a great deal of time. They require only your attention and your awareness. You *can* just flip through this book, and you may find it of some interest or entertainment. Or, you can use this book to transform your life. The power you hold is the power to decide. What is your decision? Are you ready to transform your life? Are you ready to grow? Are you ready to learn to think with the heart and love with the mind?

If so, then let's begin. Schedule 20 minutes on your calendar each morning. Begin to imagine what living life from a higher level of consciousness can be like. And enjoy!

YOUR 30-DAY WORKBOOK

Each day in the workbook has three sections that relate to the fundamentals of inner development. These are the most important elements. Each day starts with a quote either from the book *Think with the Heart / Love with the Mind* or from one of my other books or sources. Following the quote is the explanation of the image that is used for that day's study. Then I present further advice for enhancing your meditation practice, the first of the big three. If you don't have an effortless meditation practice, please visit www.HeartBasedMeditation.com and sign up for one of the trainings.

The next section is designed to enhance your development of intuition and your inner guidance system. This is key to learning to think with the heart.

Finally, the last section in each day's study has to do with restructuring the programming and patterns that exist deep in your mind. This is the work of integrating greater awareness into your functioning in all areas of life. This helps you to move toward the state of higher consciousness without getting pulled back into the old habit patterns and emotions that pull you down into identification with the ego.

These are the big three: 1) Meditation, 2) Thinking with the heart (developing intuition), and 3) Loving with the mind (reprogramming the habit patterns of the mind). In practicing these each day, you will dramatically accelerate your inner growth and development. For each day I have provided a page for you to note your discoveries and progress.

Know that what awaits you is an exciting journey. Know that you are more than you have ever imagined. Know that you are loved. Know that life can unfold in such bountiful ways that you will be forever grateful.

Love yourself, love the world, and keep your light shining brightly,

Paul

DAY 1
Quote of the Day

My seeking is coming to an end and my finding is beginning.

THE IMAGE

The image is one of an angelic being moving forward with determination, radiating both love and a clear path to the goal. Your path is becoming clearer, and you, who can hold a radiance as high as the angels, are now ready for your spiritual goals to be met. Your seeking has been noble, but it is time now that you begin to find that what you are seeking is deep within you. *[Image credit: Bruce Rolff@123RF.com]*

MEDITATION

Einstein is paraphrased as saying, "We cannot solve our problems with the same level of thinking that created them." Meditation is the key to getting to that higher state that allows your problems to be readily solved. It is where the seeking comes to finding. Meditation does take time for the change to occur. Your seeking will turn to finding, though, very soon, if you are regular with your meditation practice. Think of it like getting a good night's sleep before a big presentation or tryout. You just wouldn't consider doing things any other way. So, as you commit to this work for the next 30 days, commit also to the foundation of inner growth. Meditate twice daily for at least 20 minutes, and watch what happens. Discover what solutions you come to spontaneously over the next month. Write them down.

THINK WITH THE HEART

What you are seeking is not outside of you. It is deep within your heart. It is at the most subtle feeling level. The key to beginning to develop this awareness and the power of intuition is to begin paying attention to what you are feeling. Then ask, *"What is underneath this feeling when I feel into it even deeper?"* Spend this day, throughout the day, putting your awareness on the feeling level of life. With each feeling go deeper into a more subtle level of feeling underneath the emotion. What do you experience?

LOVE WITH THE MIND

The shift for your mind to make now is to understand that everything that you seek is ultimately within you. The first step to loving with the mind is to divorce it from the notion that success, fulfillment, love, beauty and everything else you seek is outside of you. You are the element that gives beauty its appreciation. You are that which finds your heart's fulfillment. For today, begin to affirm: *"Whether I believe it or not, my own heart holds everything I seek in life."* Repeat this affirmation throughout the day, whenever you think of it.

Notes

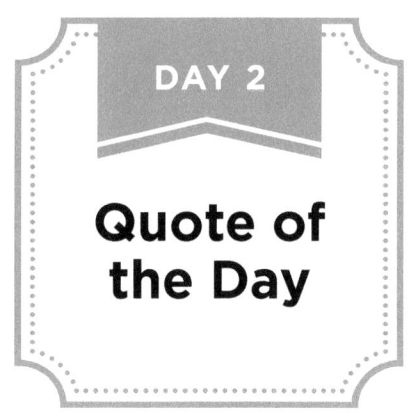

Quote of the Day — DAY 2

Meditation is the foundation of inner growth.

THE IMAGE

The image is one of the unfolding of untold light, beauty, radiance and bliss that comes with the regular practice of meditation. Reality is full of radiant colors normally unseen until you undertake inner development. *[Image credits: Tommaso Lizzul@123RF.com, Snezh@123RF.com, Bruce Rolff@123RF.com]*

MEDITATION

Meditation: Your experience is everything. What happens is that you are unable to recognize that you are progressing because you do not remember the change from the prior state. Your current state becomes your natural state. For that reason it helps to keep a meditation journal. Write out your experience. Today add 5 minutes of deep breathing before your meditation. With each inhale imagine light being pulled down from the heavens through the back of your spine. With each exhale imagine the light being pulled around and up the front of your body to your heart. Note what difference, if any, this makes in your meditation. And write it down.

THINK WITH THE HEART

Yesterday you were noticing the feeling level of life. What did you notice underneath each emotion? Was there another emotion? Or was there silence? Today again, attend to the heart space and pay attention to what arises there. Do you get a sense about anything before it happens? Do you have a feeling about what might be said by someone before they say it? Just return to the heart space and note what you feel on this day. As you meditate more, awareness of the subtle intuition of the heart will arise more and more.

LOVE WITH YOUR MIND

What if the mind were to operate from the level of peace and surrender that takes place in meditation? In meditation you let go completely. What if the mind were to let go and come to silence in activity? That which keeps you from loving with the mind is the attachment to ideas and desires. Meditation starts to train the mind to let go and accept what is. This is key to living life in peace and harmony. Make meditation the foundation of your growth by keeping your practice regular. Then, after taking the cleansing shower, don't go rolling in the mud. Let go when you think of it in activity. Ask yourself, *"Can I, on some level, start to accept what is?"* If you can change what is, then do so. If you cannot, come to peace with it. Let go. Find the peace in this moment that occurs with this letting go. And love yourself.

Notes

DAY 3
Quote of the Day

We don't solve problems — we outgrow them.

THE IMAGE

The image is one of life sprouting forth. Growth is to be honored and valued. It brings freshness and liveliness. And as you sprout forth, many of the old problems and patterns fall away spontaneously. Inner growth is one way that you solve many problems indirectly. Life sprouts from an inner core of silence. My friend, trust it, encourage it, promote it, and come to transformation beyond what you could ever imagine. *[Image credit: Natalia Zimneva@123RF.com]*

MEDITATION

What I want for you is the most powerful meditation. Preparation for meditation can be of the utmost importance. Classically the preparation for meditation was yoga asana. Your greatest growth comes with the greatest vacation your meditation brings. In other words, the deeper the relaxation and letting go that occur in meditation, the faster the growth of consciousness. In the last section, we talked about doing deep breathing before meditation. One additional preparation that does not take as much time as yoga is a special type of music called Hemi-Sync. This music uses special sound technology that causes the brainwaves to synchronize and the mind to settle. Doing five minutes of music followed by five minutes of deep breathing (with or without music) is ideal preparation for meditation. Deep meditation makes for rapid growth where many problems and challenges will simply fall off. My friend, that is my wish for you.

THINK WITH THE HEART

Many problems get worse because we overthink them. If you feel into the depth of the heart, you will find a simple clarity — a pure knowing. If you are analyzing and rethinking each problem and decision, you are giving the mind too much power. The mind can entertain anything. It can take one side of a debate and then flip to the other. It is the heart that grounds the mind. One of the fastest ways to outgrow the problems that the mind presents is to learn to surrender mental activity and let it go in favor of feeling into the heart and listening to its wisdom.

LOVE WITH THE MIND

It is time for your mind to let go of its self-judgment. Problems do not mean that you are defective. They mean that you are waking up to what is about to be transformed. This shift in perspective comes with a shift to acceptance. This is the beginning of loving with the mind. Do not judge problems. Look at any problem that you have confronted in your life and have learned from or have outgrown. Each problem is a challenge that pushes you to higher learning, greater wisdom and greater compassion. Understand that some of these problems you will solve actively, but many you will outgrow as you grow in awareness. Let yourself come into acceptance of "problems" and come to accepting and embracing both the challenge and the reality that many of these challenges will fall off as you grow. Love yourself and the challenges you have already outgrown. Sit with that — you have already outgrown many challenges. And so you shall in the future, as well.

Notes

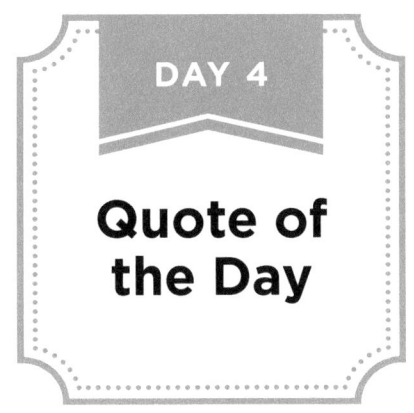

DAY 4
Quote of the Day

*When we pray, we talk to God.
When we meditate, we listen.*

— Charlie Lutes

THE IMAGE

The image is the connection to something greater and the discovery of a greater order, even in what may seem like the chaos and randomness of a cloud formation. When you discover this higher order, you begin to see the essence of the energy that underlies creation. That essence is love. When you listen to the Universe, the Divine speaks to you in multiple ways. In order to listen, you must listen with the heart. *[Image credit: Chalida Techapanupreeda @123RF.com]*

MEDITATION

Meditation does not have to be full of silence. It is the failure to let go and discharge all the energy behind the stress that stands in the way of silence. The discharging of the stress is important. It is a listening process. You allow whatever comes up to be and just let it go. This is the opposite of prayer, where you are engaging the mind and the will to speak to God and making your prayers known. Let your meditation be that time when you let go and listen to what the Universe *is,* and what it is saying.

THINK WITH THE HEART

Thinking with the heart is as much a process of listening as it is an active process of thinking. You listen to what your heart is telling you. This connects you to the depths of your soul. And this connects you to your Higher Self. Today listen well.

LOVE WITH THE MIND

Do less with the mind and more with the heart. The mind judges, criticizes and evaluates. Loving with the mind means letting go of judgments and expectations. In order to open to the love and the awesomeness of the Universe, you must let go of evaluations, judgments and expectations. Listen to the Universe and you will hear no judgment whatsoever. Today practice not judging. How do you do this? First, observe what the mind is doing without evaluation and then, when you notice the judgments coming in, let go and come back to the heart. Come back to love. Set down your gavel, do not judge, and see all with a balanced mind full of equanimity.

Notes

DAY 5
Quote of the Day

Meditation is dissolution of thoughts in Eternal awareness or Pure consciousness without objectification, knowing without thinking, merging finitude in infinity.

— Voltaire

THE IMAGE

The image represents the spiral inward as the mind lets go into the depths of meditation. The spiral inward is complex, multifaceted, and often results in a path that seems as if it is not going anywhere. Yet, the mind is eventually drawn inward toward the center — toward the pure consciousness. Here you find what you are seeking, for it is deep within you. *[Image credit: Fernando Batista@123RF.com]*

MEDITATION

I have given you two ways to improve your meditations: 1) Hemi-Sync Music; 2) Deep Breathing. While you don't try for silence in meditation, understanding the purification process and what accelerates the clearing can lead to deeper, more quiet and more profound meditations. David R. Hawkins writes: *"According to scientific findings, all thoughts are filed in the mind's memory bank under a filing system based upon the associated feeling and its finer gradations (Gray–LaViolette, 1982). They are filed according to feeling tone, not fact. Consequently, there is a scientific basis for the observation that self-awareness is increased much more rapidly by observing feelings rather than thoughts. The thoughts associated with even one feeling may literally run into the thousands.* [Hawkins, David R. (2013-08-01). Letting Go: The Pathway of Surrender (p. 34). Veritas Publishing. Kindle Edition.] The concept of one emotion creating thousands of thoughts is true of the purification process as well. A single stress may come out as hundreds of thoughts, *if* you do not process this on the level of emotion. That means discharging the energy behind the emotion and letting go of the feeling with complete awareness. Today enhance your meditations by staying completely aware of the feeling level of your experience during the day. Feel into, but do not be consumed by, emotions as they come and go throughout the entire day.

THINK WITH THE HEART

Intuition comes out of the ability to passively receive. It comes out of silence. After each meditation, sit with your eyes closed and just ask to receive whatever guidance your Higher Self has for you for that day. Write it down. As much as I long for your freedom, your fulfillment, your connection to love and life energy, your Higher Self will guide you much more quickly than I can. Do this, my friend, and life will transform.

LOVE WITH THE MIND

The key to affirmations and to reprogramming the subconscious mind is the energy of emotion you put behind the affirmation. Whether it is the energy of determination, of excitement or of love, use that energy to allow your affirmations to produce profound effects. Today use this affirmation: *"I let go and I let God."* It is really too much of a burden to try to control everything. Turn it over to the Divine and let your load be lightened.

Notes

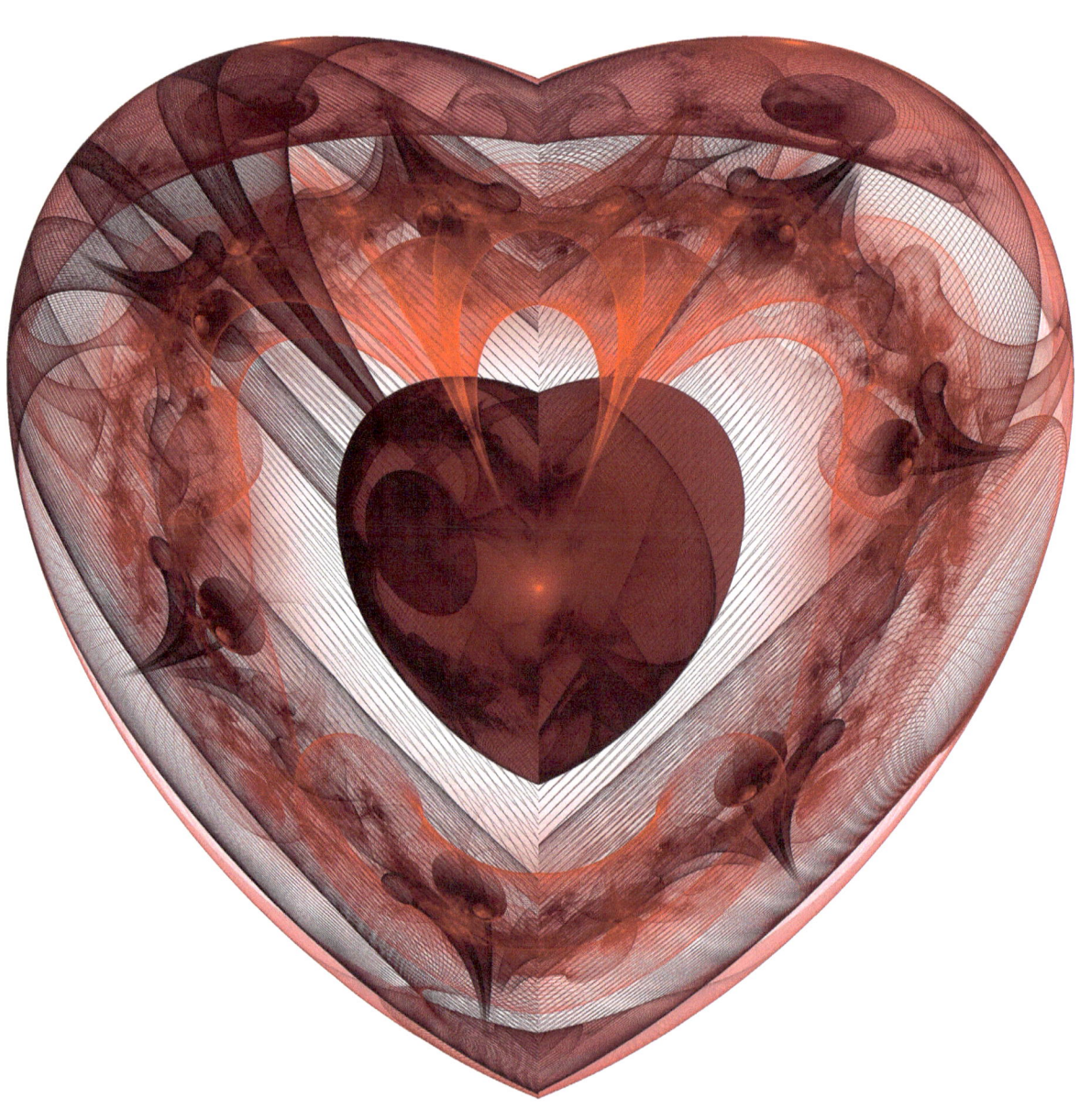

Quote of the Day

DAY 6

Love many things, for therein lies the true strength, and whosoever loves much performs much, and can accomplish much, and what is done in love is done well.

— Vincent Van Gogh

THE IMAGE

Within the heart lies the true heart — the heart that is your connection to the Divine and to your soul. The personal heart is on the surface. It experiences the hurts and infatuations, the losses and resentments, the personal connections and the personal loves and hates. Deep in the heart is the connection to the soul. Here is where divine love radiates. Here is your true home. What you seek outside of yourself lies in the true heart, deep within you. When you love from this place, there is real power and strength. What is done from this place "can accomplish much, and what is done in love is done well." *[Image credit: Olga Buiacova@123RF.com]*

MEDITATION

If you don't love meditation, you soon will, as long as you don't get into effort with it. Just accept any clouds that may be present, knowing that they will pass and the sun will come forth. Over time, with deeper experience, meditation becomes that twice-daily vacation. Give it a little more time. You will come to love it.

THINK WITH THE HEART

Too often we think of love as only relating to romantic love. You want to remember all the ways love expresses itself. You may love sports. If that is the case, the joy you feel is part of the way in which your heart experiences love. Joy is an aspect of love. When a father works to support his family, it is an expression of love. When a mother reminds her child of a homework assignment, it is an expression of caring born of love. Love and enjoyment are key components of evolution. To cultivate both intuition and the ability to think with the heart, follow your joy. "Love many things…" and with the strength and energy born of that love, decisions will be easy; courage will be easy to find; success will be easy to find; and, intuition will unfold rapidly.

LOVE WITH THE MIND

What are the blocks to your passion? What stops you from being in awe at your life? What prevents you from following your bliss? Paying attention to what others think is often a block. "What would they think if I did X, Y or Z?" Doing what you "should do" is another potential block that can be insidious. Yes, you have responsibilities. But, too often, doing what you "should" robs you of your energy, your joy and your enthusiasm. Make sure your "shoulds" are reflecting your real values and not other people's expectations (especially those of your parents). With each "should" you find yourself thinking, change it to "I choose to enjoy…" So instead of *"I should work out today,"* change it to *"I chose to enjoy working out today."* If you can't chose to enjoy it, it is probably better not to do it. It will deprive you of your life energy and your joy. It will keep your mind in a rigid pattern that doesn't allow it to love. Choose joy. Choose love. And "love many things…"

Notes

DAY 7

Quote of the Day

The dark night of the soul is really the dark night of the ego. It is the soul's daybreak!

THE IMAGE

To the extent that you resist growth and transformation, you create pain and suffering. When it is time for the soul to begin to run the show instead of the ego, then any attempt of the ego to maintain control is met with problems and disaster. The bigger the attachment, the harder the fall. Everything in one's life may seem like it is falling apart. Not everyone has to go through the dark night of the soul. For some who are learning to let go to Spirit, the transition can be more of a gray day than a dark night. The process involves allowing the dark side, the shadow or unconscious self, to become conscious. This is represented in the image by the Yin-Yang symbol made of stars. As all becomes conscious, then the light of intuition shines forth, represented by the third eye above the symbol. This process is not really one of the darkness of the soul, rather it is the darkness of the ego. Once the ego's tight grip is released the dawn of the soul's destiny can shine forth. *[Image credit: Jozef Klopacka@123RF.com]*

MEDITATION

Everyone has some resistance. Even if the dark night of the soul is the gray day of the soul, it still comes with stress as the ego learns to let go and take a backseat to the soul. Meditation resolves the stress. Meditation resolves the tension that is created by resistance. It is a practice that releases the tensions of unfulfilled desires, wants, longings and frustrations. It is a practice that releases the stress caused by impressions that have gone deep into the mind. Today before you sit to meditate, intend for grace to be a part of your path and the letting go to be easy. Remember, when we ask for consciousness, we no longer write the script — the play is directed by the Divine. May you be so graced!

THINK WITH THE HEART

Thinking with the heart means operating from this purview in all matters. Having "heartfulness for all things," including yourself, is key. Residing in the heart, thinking from there, results naturally when you stop operating from the ego. The place to start with this practice is to start loving yourself. Love your resistance to what is. Love your emotions, whatever they are. Love both your Yin and your Yang. Love that part of you that struggles so. Love that part of you that wants the best for everyone. The more you reside in love, the more the messages of the heart will become clear and the more they can guide you on your path.

LOVE WITH THE MIND

"Let go and let God," must be the attitude to help you get through the dark night of the soul. However, when you let go, understand that nature abhors a vacuum. So with the *attitude* of letting go, today add this to your affirmations: *"I embrace all the wonderful new the Divine has for me."* Make this the full affirmation that you come back to repeatedly: *"I let go and I let God, and I embrace all the wonderful new the Divine has for me."*

Notes

DAY 8
Quotes of the Day

It is not the grace of a master, nor the grace of a teacher, nor the grace of some external God that frees you. It is the grace of the purity that exists deep within your own heart.

My heart is my inner guidance system.

THE IMAGE

The beauty, complexity and depth of the heart are displayed in this image. The heart, not the brain, is the source of your wisdom. The heart knows. It teaches you and leads you on your path. If you feel off your path, then ask *"Have I really been listening to my heart?"* The heart, more than any master or teacher or guide, knows the way. God's grace needs a receiver for its transmission. Your heart is that receiver. Listen to it as much as you can.
[Image credit: Bobbie Sandlin@123RF.com]

MEDITATION

While a master or teacher can connect you to a path or a channel of consciousness, it is the grace of the Divine that frees you. Ultimately meditation is a do-it-yourself process. A meditation that emphasizes the connection to the heart offers the most direct connection to grace. Meditation affords you a way to clear the blocks to the heart and open to its grace. Commit yourself to keeping your meditation practice regular today.

THINK WITH THE HEART

Your heart is your inner guidance system. Eventually intuition can come in flashes of images and clear auditory communication. However, it is easiest to start with the feeling sense. Everyone can feel when something constricts or expands their heart. Test things using this subtle feeling sense. When you have a choice to make, does it make your heart constrict or does it feel like freedom, expansion and ease? Use this beginning sense of constriction or expansion in the heart as your practice today with each little decision you make. Understand that if you practice this, it can be the foundation for your inner guidance system.

LOVE WITH THE MIND

The mind can create anything, rationalize anything, justify anything and make anything seem good or bad. The ungrounded mind can entertain all possibilities over and over again. It is the grounding in the heart and in the value system and integrity of the individual that keeps the mind grounded and useful. Think less, listen to the heart more and turn each negative thought over to the silence. Let go of any negativity and let the heart lead the way. You are love, my friend, in your core and in your essence. Let that truth ground your mind, and be blessed.

Notes

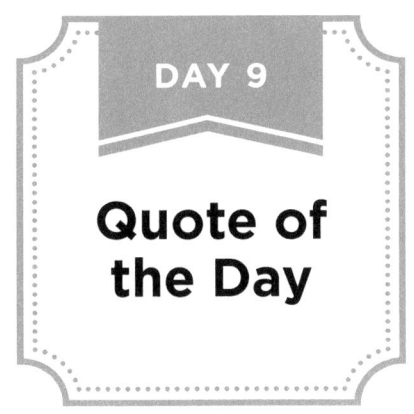

DAY 9
Quote of the Day

Growth is not a mystery, but it can result in a profoundly mystical, awe-inspired life.

THE IMAGE

As you grow and develop spiritually, the human nervous system and what it is capable of perceiving also grows. You become able to perceive energy more readily. At first, you may only sense or feel it, but eventually you will also perceive it. All of creation becomes a fascinating display of energy. *[Image credit: Nikki Zalewski@123RF.com]*

MEDITATION

The value of using a mantra for meditation is the development of subtle perception. As you become more familiar with the very subtle levels of the mantra, you will begin to develop more sensitivity to subtle energy. This does not happen overnight. It happens over time. This is one of the side benefits of mantra-based meditation.

THINK WITH THE HEART

Feeling and sensing at the subtle level requires you to get out of your head and into the finest feeling level. This is where the practice of letting go and coming into the depths of the heart on a moment-to-moment basis becomes so important. Make this your practice today outside of meditation.

LOVING WITH THE MIND

Where are you missing the awe of life? The mind thinks about 60,000 thoughts a day. The vast majority of them are the same thoughts as the day before. The mind can get lost in itself. The ability to appreciate each aspect of your existence and to take in the beauty and the awesomeness of life requires the mind to be trained. Today practice gratitude. Give gratitude for whatever you can throughout the day. Pay attention to the effects of giving gratitude on your mood and attitude. Make it an amazing, blessed day. Practicing gratitude is the perfect practice for the mind, my friend. It is a foundational practice for remembering truth and cultivating love. It is your way of blessing. Make it your habit today and every day.

Notes

DAY 10
Quote of the Day

Never lose an opportunity of seeing anything beautiful, for beauty is God's handwriting.

— Ralph Waldo Emerson

THE IMAGE

When you love with the mind, you find appreciation in everything. Your eyes see beauty everywhere. The image is one of the eye that sees beauty in everything and sees into the subtle energy of things. When you love what you are doing, when you love what is present for you, when you love with the mind, everything becomes an expression of beauty. Beauty results from appreciation, and appreciation shapes the perception. *[Image credit: Jozef Klopacka@123RF.com]*

MEDITATION

Today try resting for 5-10 minutes after your meditation. This extra rest can help to clear the windows of perception. It can help you to see more clearly and appreciate more the beauty that is present in life. For some people this practice can provide a great deal of integration and allow more of the silence of meditation to carry over into the day. It can also allow the nervous system more rest and a more gradual transition out of the meditation. These both help you to have a fresh perspective. As I found early in my meditation career, it becomes hard to maintain a negative mood when you meditate regularly. Most of the time, each meditation will wipe the slate clean.

THINK WITH THE HEART

What you see is a reflection of what you are. The beauty and appreciation that you have for things come not from your eyes, but from the quality of your heart. Cultivate a heart that finds beauty everywhere by clearing any old hurts and resentments from the heart. Let these go and feel into the depths of caring that reside in the heart. Today let yourself release and let go. With this practice you will come to find the beauty within.

LOVE WITH THE MIND

Yesterday, I emphasized the role of gratitude and the cultivation of the finer feeling levels and reprogramming the mind. Here again, an attitude that reflects heart qualities will allow the mind to be cultured and new habits to form. A quote attributed to Steven Covey is this: "Sow a thought and reap an action. Sow an action and reap a habit. Sow a habit and reap a character. Sow a character and reap a destiny." Today shift your attitude to one of appreciation. Sow thoughts of appreciation with each moment that you can remember to do so throughout the day. Take the action of sharing that appreciation, whether it be one of beauty or appreciating someone's help or support. Consider making this your habit, and it will develop into a powerful and loving character — the qualities of the enlightened soul.

Notes

DAY 11
Quote of the Day

Growth is a lot easier when it is done consciously.

THE IMAGE

The butterfly appears after a metamorphosis from a caterpillar to a deep resting state and then the full blossoming of beauty. It reminds us of the value of transformation and the awesome result. Growth in nature happens effortlessly. Humans often stand in the way of our fastest path to growth. For us, conscious growth is much easier. When you resist growth and do not undertake to engage it in a conscious way, then your soul creates painful experiences to wake you up. This is the hard way. Lessons that you suddenly seem to run into — that seem to come out of nowhere — are ways your soul is calling out for you to wake up. An easier way is to undertake conscious growth. Taking steps to develop your awareness and shift your inner programming, to let go of the habitual ways of thinking and doing, and lead with your heart, allows for a path of growth that is full of ease and grace. *[Image credit: Jozef Klopacka@123RF.com]*

MEDITATION

I have said it several times: Meditation is the foundation for inner growth. The butterfly is the perfect analogy. By going into a deep state of suspended animation, the caterpillar transforms into the butterfly. For you, going into a deep state of release, letting go and resting the mind allows you to transform your life. You come out of meditation with a clean slate, ready to allow your true essence to shine forth.

THINK WITH THE HEART

Intuition and imagination are right next to each to other in terms of function and similarity. One way to develop your visual sense of intuition is to practice working with imagery. Actively imagining something is very close to receiving intuitions that come in the form of symbols, images and "inner sight." You can use the sense of sight, the sense of sound, or the feeling sense when it comes to intuition. You can also "imagine" a sound or words and create them in the mind. These acts of creation and how you experience them are very close to how you receive intuitive guidance. The most important component of this is learning to let go and receive impressions and to know clearly when you are creating them and when you are receiving them — this is crucial to the development of intuition. Practice is also key. Intuition is a skill like any other skill. It takes practice. The practice below is one that can enhance intuition. It is best done after meditation.

Practice

1. First imagine a scene — a Christmas tree, for example.
2. Add detail to the imagination. For the Christmas tree example, add what is at the base of the tree, what is behind it, what room it is in, who is in the room with it, etc.
3. Now ask your intuition to alter the scene in some meaningful way. Let go and just allow things to happen. Don't worry about the meaning.
4. Ask your intuition if the changes in the scene have any meaning. Wait and see what comes. If there is meaning, ask what it is.
5. Don't doubt. Just receive whatever you get.

LOVE WITH THE MIND

Consciously growing means looking at all the patterns of thinking and habitual ways of reacting. It means consciously choosing to release them, reprogram them or let them be (if they are serving). Today pay attention to those areas in which you fall into negative thinking. Understand that in order to think negatively you need to *suppress* the positive. Pay attention to the ways in which you suppress the positive. Write these down. Then make a conscious choice to embrace the positive the next time the thoughts arise.

Notes

Quote of the Day

Cease trying to work everything out with your minds. It will get you nowhere. Live by intuition and inspiration and let your whole life be Revelation.

— Eileen Caddy

THE IMAGE

The crystal ball has long represented intuiting the future. It symbolizes the crystal clarity with which you can see when you fully develop your intuition. Your intuition carries greater wisdom than your intellect. Trying to work things out with the mind usually leads to less clarity and more confusion. The mind can entertain anything and make the good seem bad and the bad seem good. The heart, on the other hand, knows. *[Image credit: Martin Konopka @ 123RF.com]*

MEDITATION

As you learn to let go in meditation, you come to realize that the mind can be engaged or can be let go of. Today after your meditation, see if throughout the day you can let go of the mind, even for a couple of seconds. Use that silence to feel into the heart and see what sense of things comes from that.

THINK WITH THE HEART

Continue to practice with the active versus passive imagination exercise that you did yesterday. Feel into the receptive mode. Do not question what comes, except to ask your Higher Self for clarification. The point of the exercise is to get familiar with the feeling of receptivity and how intuition comes to you. This state is the gateway to living the life of Revelation that Eileen Caddy speaks of.

LOVE WITH THE MIND

Today again, I will remind you of this quote: "Sow a thought and reap an action. Sow an action and reap a habit. Sow a habit and reap a character. Sow a character and reap a destiny." With each thought, understand that you are creating your future destiny. What thought will you sow? Try to tap into excitement and enthusiasm today, rather than sowing thoughts of struggle and hardship. Everything around you is in a dynamic state of creation. Everything is constantly unfolding. How will you unfold? Let go into the silence when the thoughts are negative. Plant positivity with your thoughts and act on them. They will become your destiny.

Notes

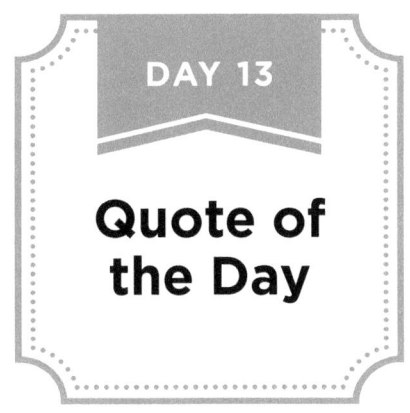

Quote of the Day

When you live in the fullness of love, then you are truly happy.

THE IMAGE

The heart is composed of red cloth arranged with waving folds. Out of simple fabric, we can create and express love. Like this, in life, we can create and live in the fullness of love. This is the source of true happiness. Live that. *[Image credit: Inara Prusakova @ 123RF.com]*

MEDITATION

The value of using a mantra is that it creates awareness on the finest, subtlest level of life. This is where intention operates. When you have a subtle intention and turn it over to the Divine, then manifestation becomes effortless, powerful and profound. Today just prior to meditating have the intention to live in the fullness of love. Feel that intention as a subtle notion, and then let it go as you start your meditation. Then allow this practice to unfold in your life.

THINK WITH THE HEART

Remember that for each individual there will be a particular sense that dominates with regard to intuition. You may have struggled with visualizations or they may have been easy for you. For some the feeling sense is more available than the visual sense. What is important is the recognition of receptivity and the openness to receiving. This is where anchoring any intuition practice in the heart can be of value. Return to the heart whenever you receive an intuition and let the heart sense verify it with a feeling of expansion ("yes") or a feeling of contraction ("no"). For some, it will be a feeling of "settledness" versus a feeling of uneasiness. Come to know the way your heart can verify the images, voices or feelings that present themselves to you throughout the day.

LOVE WITH THE MIND

Sometimes the most important thing you can do to further your growth is find the right question. This leads to the fastest growth. It furthers your path. Look at the ways in which you are not happy, then ask this question: *"What would love do?"* As you feel into this question, it will lead the mind to the greatest happiness. Remember it, use it and let it lead you every day. Love, my friend, will lead you to your happiness.

Notes

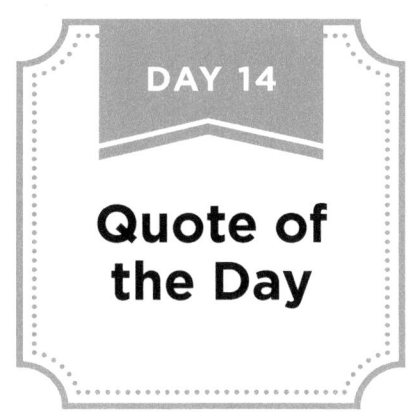

DAY 14

Quote of the Day

Loving with the mind means that you have faith that life will deliver to you exactly what you came here to experience.

THE IMAGE

The image is one of a tree growing in the shape of a heart. You can see this as just a tree in a field, or you can see a heart as a symbolic expression of love being reflected back to you in nature. When you have faith that life is unfolding exactly as it was meant to, then your perception changes. You embrace what is present, and you see love everywhere. *[Image credit: Maximsamos@123RF.com]*

MEDITATION

Starting the mantra from the heart — imagining it comes from that place rather than the throat or the head — this is a key to Heart-based Meditation. You need only start the mantra at the beginning of the meditation. Then let go. Overtime, this creates a settledness in the mind at the start of meditation. The heart is an anchor you settle into. From this grounded space, you can feel into the knowing that all is well. Life is unfolding perfectly as it was meant to unfold.

THINK WITH THE HEART

Find the place in your heart that feels most settled, most safe, and most secure. Find the place of pure knowing and pure love. If you feel past the romance, past the human hurts and vulnerabilities, you come to a place that is solid — a place of love, warmth, caring and compassion. This place of solid strength and knowing is the place to return to again and again until it becomes home.

LOVE WITH THE MIND

Review the section in the book *Think with the Heart / Love with the Mind* that is entitled "Your Soul's Permission." (It is on page 80 in the paperback version.) Use this affirmation today: *"Everything is perfect just as it is, no matter how I may feel about it at first glance. Everything is in Divine Order."*

Notes

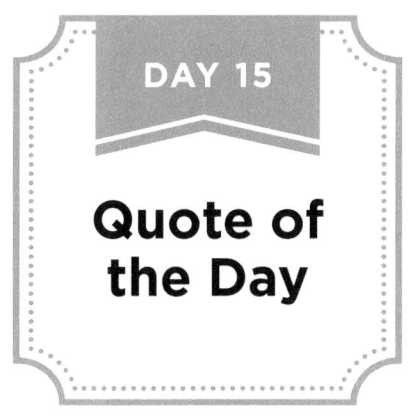

DAY 15

Quote of the Day

Well begun is half done.

— Aristotle

THE IMAGE

Today's image is cheering in victory. You have overcome the greatest hurdle. You are more than half done. Celebrate! *[Image credit: RCaucino@123RF.com]*

MEDITATION

If well begun is half done, then, with the start that you have had, you are almost done. The hardest parts are over. It is all downhill now. Today is a day of reflection. What have you noticed with your meditation practice? What experiences have you had? How is it different now? What has worked for you? Continue to meditate as usual, but afterward, write down what you have noticed so far.

THINK WITH THE HEART

Just like for meditation, today is a day of reflection on what you have discovered about intuition, about the deeper parts of your own heart, and about the wisdom and love that is unfolding at the core of your being. Reflect back over the last 15 days. What have you discovered? What are you drawn to? What wisdom has really rung true for you? Take time today to write it out. It will be valuable documentation that you can return to in the future. It will inspire you on your path, if not today, someday in the future.

LOVE WITH THE MIND

There is nothing harder to change than a habit. Most of thinking is a habit. If you have been able to change anything with the way you think — bravo! Take time and write down what is different for you now. Congratulations! Even if you have just tried and not noticed much, that will restructure your subconscious mind. So, well done YOU!

Notes

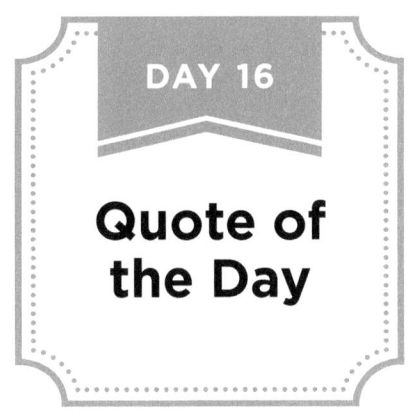

Quote of the Day

What a different world it would be if people only knew that whatever they thought or did or felt was forever written in the ethers for anyone to see.

THE IMAGE

The many selves or masks of the persona are displayed. Personality comes from the Latin word *persona* meaning mask. The Greeks wore different masks during their plays to represent different characters. We do the same. This is mostly driven by unconscious habit and by the illusion that we are separate and isolated. Nothing is really private. The many masks are seen as well as what is hidden underneath. Whether we know it or not, whether others know it or not, our thoughts and feelings affect others. Those who are sensitive can pick up on what is going on inside of us. Let go of the illusion and know that hiding doesn't work. Authenticity does. *[Image credit: Jozef Klopacka@123RF.com]*

MEDITATION

Today take the next step in your meditation practice. If you have the time and your meditations have been going smoothly (that means, not creating a lot of release of emotion and/or sleepiness during the day), then consider adding 5 more minutes to your meditation time, morning and evening. This will add more clarity and help you to experience sooner the reality of the interconnectedness of all of life.

THINK WITH THE HEART

To think with the heart, you will be well served by sharing what is in your heart and releasing it. It is often unprocessed and unresolved emotional energy that blocks the intuition and the experience of love. Be kind, be gentle, but be authentic and release what needs to be released. If it is uncomfortable to do this with others, then isolate yourself in a room and speak it outloud. Express it, so that the energy of the emotion is discharged and released. Both speaking it and also using the body in expressing it aids the release. Don't get lost it in. You don't need to encourage going deeper into the emotion. Just observe it —feel it, express it and let it go. As you observe it — not getting lost in it — the energy and clarity will start to shift, and you will find the release has enlivened you. This will pave the way to greater love and clearer intuition.

LOVE WITH THE MIND

Remember that what we think impacts others. Understand that, like a radio transmitter, this energy of thought impacts your environment and all of those around you. Uplifting thoughts uplift and attract others to you. Negative thinking pulls others down and tends to repel them, unless they have a need to try to help you. Hurtful, harmful, angry thoughts are also felt, even when not expressed. Understand that whatever you do, whatever you think, you have done this to yourself. You reap the energy of it in its karmic return. Whatever you do, you have done it to yourself. So be mindful of your thoughts today. When they turn to negativity, turn to observing your breath. And then let the negativity go and shift to the positive. You can always find something positive to think about others. Always.

Notes

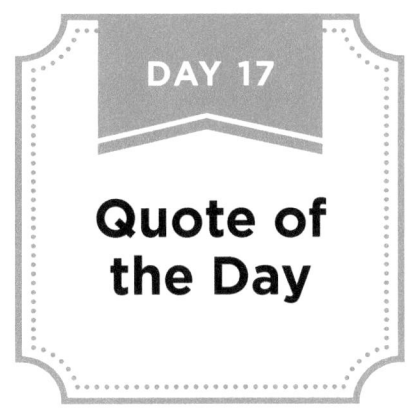

Quote of the Day

Forgive and let go. Then all freedom dawns and you come to know pure love.

THE IMAGE

Angels fly because they take themselves lightly. When you free yourself from the bondage of resentment, anger, retribution, victimhood, blame, recrimination and powerlessness, then your heart can soar with the angels. Your heart is connected upward like the image. It longs to be free. That freedom comes when you forgive and let go. *[Image credit: Bruce Rolf@123RF.com]*

MEDITATION

Meditation is a training to let go. Forgiveness is simply the process of giving over to something greater than yourself. In meditation you give over the process to something greater than yourself. You can turn it over to the Divine, to the angels, to a higher or more noble aspect of yourself. You let go and with that all freedom dawns.

THINK WITH THE HEART

It is your mind that hangs on so desperately to the past and to the resentments and injustices that have been rendered unto you. The deeper heart does not know the past. It does not know the concept of recrimination. It does not know how to resent. It is innocent. It seeks unity in all things. It knows only love. To think with the heart means to let go of the thoughts and the superficial levels of the heart that hold a grudge and that live in fear of yet more hurt. To think with the heart means to take your awareness beyond time and to reside in the present now and the bliss that is present in any moment. It is available to you. You must only forgive, let go and clear the way to the true heart.

LOVE WITH THE MIND

The mind will hang — even become addicted to — the little payoffs that come from resentment and an unforgiving nature. The ego likes to find itself righteous, and it likes to find others "wrong." It likes to feel the comfort of others who agree that it has been wronged. The ego can even become more grandiose, condescending to forgive others for their wrongs. This is not forgiveness. This is a holding onto the victim role, and making oneself out to be gracious in saying, "It's okay. I forgive you." The energy is still held. True forgiveness doesn't hold to the wrong. It doesn't make the other person bad and you good. When you truly forgive, you let it go completely. There is no victim, there is no wrong, and the past is done. Loving with the mind means coming to this state where you can truly let all the emotion and all the evaluation and judgment go. It is the mind that is so flexible and innocent that events are like drawing with your finger in the air. The ego draws with a finger in uncured concrete. Practice today turning everything over to the Divine and coming into the bliss of your own heart. Come to love. Let resentments go. Let go of the impressions that events have made. Give it over. This is the practice of forgiveness. Make it your practice today and as often as you can remember to do so.

Notes

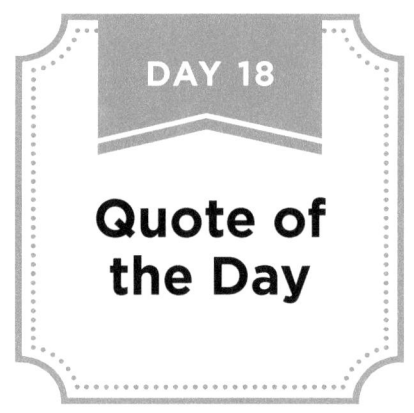

DAY 18

Quote of the Day

The mind is a wonderful tool and a horrible master.

THE IMAGE

The mind is amazing in its complexity and what it can create and conceive of. It can go down all sorts of portals and get lost in circles. The image depicts this complexity and the great variety that sits at your fingertips when you turn our attention to creative thought. It also depicts how you (the eye that witnesses all this) can get overshadowed by the mind's creations. *[Image credit: Bruce Rolf@123RF.com]*

MEDITATION

As you learn to let go in meditation, you come to realize that the mind can be more of a tool than anything else. You do not have to be identified with the mind. It is the silent witness that will develop into your true sense of self. While you are very identified with our emotions, you can get lost in your thoughts. Meditation allows you to let go of identification and discover who you really are.

THINK WITH THE HEART

Today instead of deciding even small things like what you will eat for breakfast, turn your attention to the heart space. Feel into the heart with each possibility. How does it feel? Does it cause a warmth to arise? Does it feel drawn to it? Does it feel expansive and free? Does it feel settled and solid? These are all ways in which the heart is telling you YES. If instead it feels repelled or contracts or feels unsettled, unattracted, cold or resistant, that would be a NO. Think with the heart today in making even the small decisions. It will take you out of the tyranny of the mind.

LOVE WITH THE MIND

You use the mind to calculate. But no one would want to be compulsively calculating all day. This is the situation for most humans. The mind is compulsively processing without restraint, often carrying you into dark alleys. A great quote comes from the movie *Just Like Heaven* with Mark Ruffalo playing a man who has isolated himself after the loss of his wife. His psychiatrist friend says to him, "That mind of yours is a dangerous neighborhood. You shouldn't go there alone." The mind can carry you away into darkness, as it can entertain any idea and rationalize anything. It is a horrible master. If in trying to make a decision you have gone back and forth listing all the pros and cons and ending up even more uncertain, you have experienced the problem of letting the mind run the show. The function of the mind ultimately is for you to find joy, compassion, understanding and love. It is for you to create even greater joy, even more wonderful creations, and even greater love. Today think less. Let your heart be your guide. Use the mind to love and find joy. Otherwise, let it go back to silence.

Notes

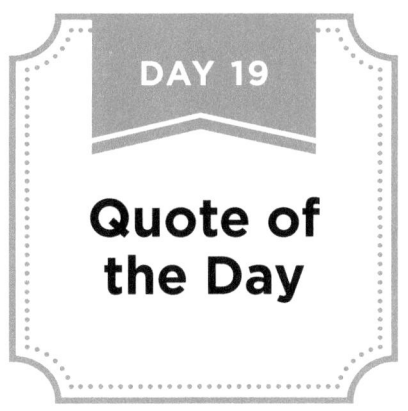

DAY 19
Quote of the Day

Love heals and paves the way to wholeness.

THE IMAGE

The shapes are beginning to come together, and like cells organizing to heal a wound, they are beginning to form a beautiful curved wholeness. The image is not complete. The process has not come to an end. Yet, you can find beauty in what is unfolding and be excited about the beauty yet to come. *[Image credit: Fernanda Batista@123RF.com]*

MEDITATION

Meditation is the fastest way to connect with the source of healing. When you go deep into letting go and into relaxation in meditation, your physiology reaches a state of rest that is often deeper than deep sleep. In that complete state of rest, the body heals. In reaching the state of pure consciousness, the stresses that have gone deep into the mind heal. Today in your meditation practice, take time to make a good transition from the busy-ness of the day. Do deep breathing before meditation to come to a deeper state of relaxation to start with. Then turn your attention to the heart space — begin meditation and come to wholeness.

THINK WITH THE HEART

Make it your habit to come to the heart and to foster love. Love yourself, and you will naturally come to love others. Don't love yourself, and you will eventually start to treat others in unloving ways. Loving yourself has nothing to do with thinking highly of yourself, with egoism or narcissism. It has to do with deep acceptance and compassion for yourself. Practice this compassion, forgiveness, acceptance and understanding. The more it becomes your way of relating to yourself, the more it will foster that healing love. Love heals all things. It is the greatest power in the universe. And it is given to you with the wonderful gift of a human heart. Today come to the heart, and find that love and compassion. It is your gateway to wholeness. Be blessed.

LOVE WITH THE MIND

The nature of the mind is such that you can choose where to put your focus. Today focus on healing those self-critical patterns by sending loving thoughts with your mind. While it is powerful to be able to speak it out, just thinking, "I love you" is a powerful healing tool. Use the mind today to say, "*I love you*" to yourself as often as you can remember. You may not feel it. Notice the resistance and what it may be telling you. And push through anyway. You will have time later to unwind the resistance. Or it may just unwind itself as you proceed with loving yourself with your mind.

Notes

DAY 20

Quote of the Day

As you develop your internal guidance system, you will find the guru within.

THE IMAGE

The guru within will usually appear first as light and energy, often with a vivid and beautiful color. Sometimes the guru within appears as just a white light in the beginning. Sometimes the guru within starts as just a feeling sense of being guided. However it may come for you, be easy with it. This image represents the light of the guru within. *[Image credit: Sakkmersterke@123RF.com]*

MEDITATION

You can't find the guru within unless you turn within. Meditation is the key to finding that internal guidance system. Often this comes with the opening of the third eye. It is important not to force this. Trying to concentrate or visualize the light in meditation can create headaches and pressure on the forehead. Sometimes, even if you are not concentrating, this type of pressure can develop as the third eye begins to open. If that is the case, it will soon pass. As it begins to open you will often start to have more refined perception and may begin to see the colors and energies of our inner guides.

THINK WITH THE HEART

The heart has a wisdom that the mind cannot attain to. The heart is connected to the soul. It has connections both with the lower and higher chakras. It also connects to the Divine Heart. Thus, it has access to much more than the mind. In all that is to be as you grow and develop in consciousness, understand that the path is not tread in miles — it is coming to the truth of your own heart. In the past, spiritual development depended on gurus, masters and teachers. In this age, knowledge is to be widespread and available. It is to be readily accessible. The age of gurus is past. You will find the guru within. The first step is listening with the heart. Today pay particular attention to what feels in alignment with your heart and to what feels like a signal that you are off track.

LOVE WITH THE MIND

Love yourself. You are an amazing being. You have the capacity to know truth, to live love, and to grow beyond your wildest imagination. The mind transformed paves the path to knowing the wisdom of the heart. The transformation comes through self love. Let yourself continue today with the practice of saying to yourself, *"I love you."* See where it leads.

Notes

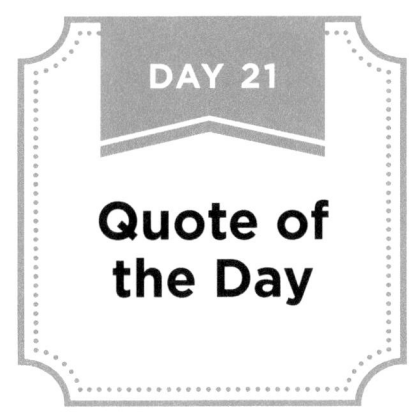

DAY 21
Quote of the Day

We cannot find a way out of suffering until we find a pathway to the true heart.

THE IMAGE

When you are disconnected from our inner wisdom you can feel desolate. The image shows a lack of life except for a tree far off in the distance. The mind can keep you trapped and rob you of life force. It can turn the ground into stormy seas and rob you of any clarity regarding the way home. *[Image credit: Harshvardhan@123RF.com]*

MEDITATION

Remember the heart is the fulcrum between the upper spiritual energy centers (chakras) and the lower, ego-centered chakras. It connects heaven and earth. With your meditation it is important that you ground into and center in the heart space, *before* you begin the meditation. You don't want to focus in the meditation. You don't want to control the process. It is important though that you start the process by turning your attention to the heart space. This helps to forge a centering and a clearing that assists you in finding a way to the true heart during our daily life.

THINK WITH THE HEART

Today observe the distinction between the true heart and the surface clouds that obscure the heart. The clouds get you lost in feelings of distrust, hurt and resentment. The clouds take you from your true innocent loving self and tell you to be cautious and not to ever trust again. Or they can lead you into making relationships and people more glamorous and romantic than they are. Pay close attention today to the surface level of the heart and the solid, deep core of the heart. Learn to discriminate between the two. Write down the differences you observe. Living more in the core of the heart will lead you out of suffering and will connect you to pure intuitive guidance.

LOVE WITH THE MIND

The mind makes things complex. Out of disappointment in the world, in God or in a person, philosophers have created whole systems of nihilistic thought that disparages life and creation. Had the hurt to the heart that was experienced healed, the whole series of thoughts and the whole system of philosophy would never have been necessary. That which keeps you in complexity and suffering is not being able to surrender the beliefs, the thoughts and the mental patterns that arise out of the unhealed places in the heart. Today, become aware of any mental negativity. Write it down. Then see if you can trace it back to some emotion, wound or stress that underlies it. Release the thoughts and just be with the feeling for a bit. See if it doesn't start to change as you just feel it. Then affirm, "*I am whole. I forgive. I give this over. I am whole.*"

Notes

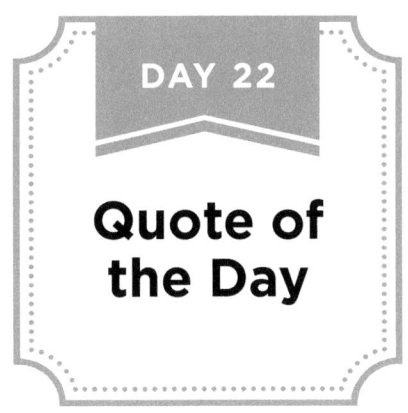

DAY 22
Quote of the Day

Faith is confidence in the unknown.

THE IMAGE

The beautiful flower shines forth its beauty without knowing what will happen. What will happen is not known. It shines forth anyway. It has confidence in the process of unfolding. It has confidence in the unknown and just shines its beauty for all to see. *[Image credit: Isoga@123RF.com]*

MEDITATION

When you let go in meditation, you are practicing faith. You are practicing having complete confidence in the unknown and simply trusting what will come. This is not an unnatural, difficult struggle. It is something you do every day when you fall asleep. In order to fall asleep, you have to let go. You have to trust that what is unknown and will transpire is all good. Then you are able to let go and fall into sleep. If you can remember the feeling of letting go and of sinking deeper into relaxation that happens with sleep, you can harness that feeling. This is exactly the feeling of letting go. This is exactly what is designed to happen in meditation. Take the plunge. Accept that you have always had the capacity to have faith in the unknown. Today in your meditation attend to this deepest relaxation and the letting go that is inspired by the practice.

THINK WITH THE HEART

What is the feeling of faith? What is the feeling that all is well? Where does this deep peace reside? Find this in your heart. Appreciate that this is what the heart is capable of. Watch the quality of thoughts that arise when you are in this state of faith and peace. This is thinking with the heart.

LOVE WITH THE MIND

This is easy to do. Remind yourself that nothing can happen to you without your soul's permission. Everything (and that means every single thing) is designed for your growth and highest development. Either you are clearing a debt (a good thing) or you are facing a challenge to develop a strength or a wisdom. Whatever it is, it is good. When you think like this, then it is easy to have confidence in the unknowns. They are all good. Today shift your perspective and focus on this. Remind yourself, *"Everything happens for my good. I have faith in the unknown."*

Notes

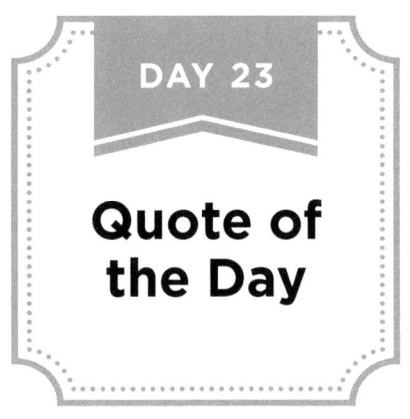

DAY 23

Quote of the Day

Consciousness heals.

THE IMAGE

The image is a cross formed from energy, almost like a quantum field pattern of the atom. The cross is symbolic of the horizontal earth being infused with consciousness from the heavens (the vertical line of spirit descending through the horizontal material world). Consciousness works at the quantum level to transform and to enliven. It is the source of the life force and the source of healing. It creates wholeness. *[Image credit: Robert Zahler@123RF.com]*

MEDITATION

Meditation aids the healing process by providing the physiology with deep rest. It gives the mind a rest as well. This is rest that is often deeper than deep sleep. Did you ever have a night when you felt like you were busy thinking all night long? You were. This is why meditation can provide even deeper rest than sleep. Doctors will tell you to rest when you are sick. Rest is an important part of allowing the healing process. But it is only one part. Another part of the process is the holistic organizing power of pure consciousness. In touching that level in mediation, you create wholeness and restore the vibrancy and the intelligent organization of the cells and their intricate, interconnected functions.

THINK WITH THE HEART

Consciousness heals on all levels, not just the physical. It heals the heart and the emotions. Putting your attention on an emotion and not entertaining the thoughts that come up, rather just dissipating the energy of the emotion, allows what underlies it to be released and to heal. This happens when you put our attention or your awareness on the feeling without getting into the thoughts about it. Thoughts just glue the energy to you. Awareness allows the energy to flow and to dissipate. This clears the way for a different feeling or emotion to come forth, and so the process continues until we come to peace. Practice just sitting in awareness of your emotions today — not feeding them with thoughts and stimulation. Let awareness heal and see what happens.

LOVE WITH THE MIND

Bringing the spiritual into the material means bringing heightened awareness to the programming that exists in each of the chakras, particularly the first through fourth chakras. These chakras anchor the mental patterns around security, emotions, wealth, sexuality, self-esteem, connection and personal love. Loving with the mind occurs when you bring awareness and higher vibration to each of these. How much of your thinking is driven by the need for certainty and security? How much of your thinking is a distraction from emotion and what you are feeling? How much of your thinking is centers on your worthiness? Bringing greater awareness to each of these areas is a task that takes much more than a day. Today, pick just one area, sit with it, and ask yourself, *"What would love do?"* What would be the most loving expression of this need? How might love fulfill here? Just the awareness itself will help the mind to transform. And if you have great success, then go ahead and pick some other areas in the coming weeks and months.

Notes

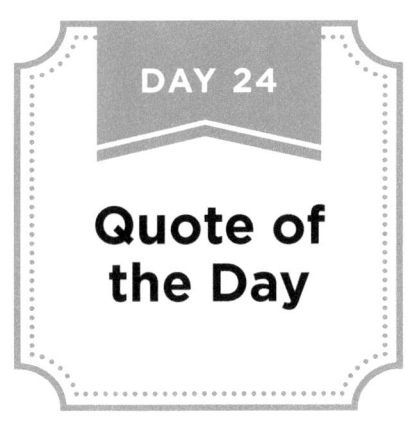

DAY 24
Quote of the Day

Our path to freedom is to learn to think with the heart and love with the mind.

THE IMAGE

The freedom of the heavens portrays the kingdom of heaven you find within, when you learn to think with the heart and love with the mind. *[Image credit: Lilkar @123RF.com]*

MEDITATION

You have almost made it. Less than a week to go before you have completed the entire 30 days. At this point be comfortable with whatever experience you've had, and just appreciate yourself for the efforts you have made. They are seeds that will sprout and grow abundant crops. Enjoy your practice today!

THINK WITH THE HEART

Honor your blessed heart today! It is such a gift. It is the treasure that will lead you to experience heaven on earth. Give thanks for it. Treasure it. And be blessed.

LOVE WITH THE MIND

Rest your mind today. It has been going through so much restructuring and reorganizing. Understand that if you push too hard, too fast, the subconscious mind can rebel. Just rest and don't think so much today.

Notes

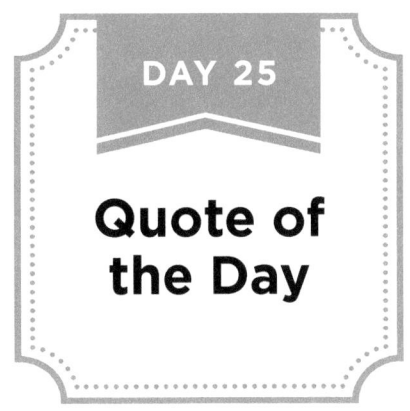

DAY 25
Quote of the Day

When you grow and evolve, then you live in love. And you know you are love.

THE IMAGE

The budding flower expresses nature's love and beauty. It is the result of growth. The plant needs to grow and develop the bud before it can develop the bloom. When you grow, you come to express all of your true nature. At the core you are love and beauty, and just as the flower blooms and expresses nature's love and beauty, so do you. Be blessed with that on this day. *[Image credit: Romasph@123RF.com]*

MEDITATION

Living in love is living the pure innocence that you reach in the process of letting go. In that process, you come to acknowledge our true nature as witness to all that unfolds. A scripture says, "Most certainly I tell you, unless you turn, and become like little children (innocent), you will in no way enter into the Kingdom of Heaven." The Kingdom of Heaven is that love that you are. It is what is experienced here on earth when you grow and evolve. Innocence is the requirement. Letting go is the way. Just accept whatever comes with today's meditation. There is nothing to achieve.

THINK WITH THE HEART

Feel love today. It is the essence of who you are. Let go, let be, let love be. Come to what is at the core of the depth of the heart. Live that, and you live in the field of love — in love in all ways.

LOVE WITH THE MIND

Know you are love. Recreate the concept of who you are with this affirmation, *"I am love."* Use this affirmation throughout the day. Understand that is your essence. Let go of analyzing. Come to the innocence that can use the mind to find awe in the amazing beauty of creation. From that perspective affirm the truth, *"I am love."*

Notes

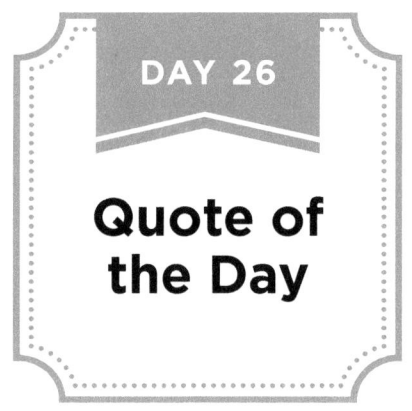

DAY 26

Quote of the Day

What I resist, persists. What I fear, I become.

THE IMAGE

The image is one of hardened crystallization. It represents the hardening that can take place in the body when you resist things emotionally and energetically. That which you resist crystallizes and contracts your energy and your heart. *[Image credit: 3quarks@123RF.com]*

MEDITATION

Today put your attention on going with the flow. Take a look at the lyrics of the Beatles song *Across the Universe:* "Words are flowing out like endless rain into a paper cup; They slither wildly as they slip away across the universe." Let yourself be in total nonresistance and allow whatever comes up in meditation to "slip away across the universe."

THINK WITH THE HEART

Don't hold on to grudges. Don't hold on to resentments. Don't hold on to fears. These block the path to the true heart. These stand in the way. How do you let go of these? First, feel where they reside in your body energetically. Feel into them. Honor them, as they served you in the past. Let yourself experience them *without* thought. The thoughts will just make them persist. Just feel into them and then see how your body or your voice wants to dissipate the energy that is there. Move your body, use your voice and move the energy of the emotion out. Stay centered in witnessing the emotion and the energy. Watch and observe what happens as the energy is released. As you observe them, you will see or sense them melt away. Then find the love that is underneath. There is no need to hold on to anything. Let go of resistance and let go of fear — they may have served you well in the past, but now you can honor them and no longer be attached to them.

LOVE WITH THE MIND

The realizations that come when you let go can be profound. The mind does not need to continue to stimulate the emotions and then try to resist their natural expression and dissipation. The mind will come up with stories and rationalizations, with models of justice and injustice to reinforce the feelings that are stuck. If the thought is not loving, if the thought does not accept life as it is, then you are in resistance. This dampens the life force and blocks the flow of emotion. Observe your thoughts. Dismantle the notions of victimhood, of fairness and of entitlement. These will only keep you in pain. Love yourself. Love that you have made it through the pain and that you are now here, alive and able to grow and thrive. Turn your thoughts to love and let go.

Notes

Quote of the Day

True faith brings a confidence that you are exactly where you need to be and that nothing can happen to you without your soul's permission.

THE IMAGE

The image is one of the soul guided to the highest heavens by the light of the soul in the depths of the heart. This is what you attain to when you develop true faith. Heaven is not above you. It is within you. You attain to heaven when you come to faith that you are exactly where you need to be, and that nothing can happen to you without your soul's permission. *[Image Credit: Bruce Rolff @ 123RF.com]*

MEDITATION

Today before you meditate be sure to do deep breathing. On the inhale imagine the light coming down your crown, down the back of your spine. This will ground you before meditation and allow you that sense of deep peace. This is the basis of true faith. Faith is more than an idea. It is a grounding into peace, knowing that all is happening exactly as it is supposed to happen.

THINK WITH THE HEART

"Faith, hope and love, these three remain, but of these three love is the greatest," said St. Paul. But the other two are pretty great in and of themselves. Faith *allows* love to be known. Faith allows you to open to love and light. It says, "I accept that I may not know what will happen, but I do know I will be okay. And I do know that everything that happens to me is fully for my good, whether it is to be a clearing of a karmic debt, the opportunity to love some aspect of myself that was hidden in the unconscious (hidden in the shadow), or whether it is an opportunity for me to find the strength and courage to confront and change the world." Faith creates the knowing that the unknown is not to be feared. It creates the confidence and the safety for love to shine. Today rest in that confidence and feel your heart blossom.

LOVE WITH THE MIND

Significant reprogramming of the mind is needed for you to take 100 percent responsibility for all that happens to you and all that you project onto the world with our assumptions, judgments and evaluations. Today, let your affirmation be, *"I trust love. I know all is unfolding exactly as is best for me, whether I see it easily or not."* Trust love. Return the mind to the place of trust. And feel the ease that results.

Notes

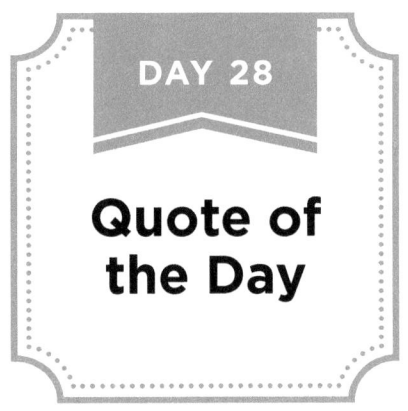

DAY 28

Quote of the Day

When I am in the flow of love, I heal.

THE IMAGE

The beautiful calm waters bridged by the rainbow of light... This image evokes the peacefulness of calm water and the flow of beauty and light. When you find this peacefulness in your heart, then love can flow easily. It brings forth treasures and rainbows because love heals. *[Image credit: Dmitry Kushch@123RF.com]*

MEDITATION

When you are in meditation, when you are practicing Heart-based Meditation, you are in the flow of love. This style of meditation places you solidly in the flow of life, and encourages your most profound practice of pure acceptance. Whatever comes up, is what the nervous system needs. Simply allow it. Accept it and continue with the flow. Honor yourself, dear friend, for this. You are affecting many more lives than just your own when you meditate. Let yourself be honored. Let yourself be loved. And let the contact with your true self bring forth healing as you connect to the source of healing and the source of love.

THINK WITH THE HEART

Healing is not something you do with the mind. It is the heart that heals. It is love that heals. Being in the flow of love enlivens and rejuvenates every cell in your body. Reinforce that practice where you bring your attention to the heart. Today, throughout the day, bring your awareness to the heart and let the love that resides in the heart flow. Whether you express it outwardly — loving life, loving the weather or loving beauty — or if you choose to love yourself, honoring all that goodness that you are and all that you have done, stay in the flow of love. Why? Because love heals.

LOVE WITH THE MIND

The mind is not the enemy of the heart. It can be its good friend. The mind works naturally on the same principle of love as does the heart. It goes from place to place seeking greater fascination, greater interest, greater beauty, greater pleasure, greater excitement, greater reward. Even a depressing line of thought reflects either a fascination or some reward or payoff that keeps you stuck there. To stay in the negative requires you to suppress the positive. Yet, in its pure innocent nature the mind seeks something more pleasurable. It seeks something that it *loves*. That is why scientists say they love science. That is why artists say they love art. The mind, when it is deprogrammed from all the unconscious payoffs and negativity, naturally seeks what it loves. It flows with the love and that love is healing. Today let the mind flow to positivity and what it *truly* enjoys. This is when you heal the fastest, when you love the most.

Notes

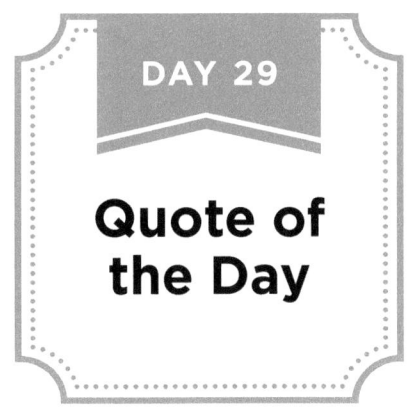

DAY 29
Quote of the Day

What you seek is already within you.

THE IMAGE

The eye looks to the angel above and it looks to the wise monk below. There appears to be light radiating from both. The eye looks outward for the light. But the light, the ability to perceive and the ability to recognize the Pure Light is not outside. It is not in the angel or in the monk. It is within the perceiver. What you seek is already within you. It only awaits your opening to it. *[Image credit: Bruce Rolf@123RF.com]*

MEDITATION

Understand that the unfolding of reality comes gradually for most of us. That means that the first thing you begin to notice in meditation is a few moments of silence or stillness. This seems pleasant enough in the beginning, but you get used to it. What you don't realize is that this is the beginning of the unfolding of what you seek. It is your first glimpse of it. Within it, all bliss, all love, all fulfillment, all creativity and true enlightenment resides. Don't force it. It will unfold over time. Just continue your regular meditation practice — the silence will transform and it will transform *you.*

THINK WITH THE HEART

Love that you have sought something more in life. Love that you have sought something higher. Love that you sought growth, freedom and enlightenment. And love the one who has been seeking. What you seek is the light. The light is not outside of you. It *is* you. Not the personality. Not the body. The real you. The one who experiences everything. You are the light. You are love. You are light *and* love. And that is what you seek. You can't know this on just a mental level. The way of knowing this is coming to love over and over again, until it is lights up every experience you have. You are what you have been seeking. This wisdom resides in your heart. Reside there today, and let it speak to you. Let it assure you that the seeking has ended, and you have found home.

LOVE WITH THE MIND

Let go of the striving now. Let the mind rest. Reassure it that it has done its job. You are coming home now. Today let this be your affirmation, *"I rest in my heart. I rest in my home. I am the light. I am love."* When you use affirmations be sure you feel into them. The more energy behind them, the faster they sink in. Don't let the mind get into analyzing if they are true or if they might be better said another way or if they make you feel awkward. Just put the energy into them, and they will be heard by your subconscious, even if you consciously feel awkward. *"I rest in my heart. I rest in my home. I am the light. I am love."* And so it is.

Notes

DAY 30
Quote of the Day

Live love and keep your light shining brightly. And may you be so blessed.

THE IMAGE

The image says it all. It is what is truly in my heart and what wants to be communicated to yours. You have made it through the 30 days. And if you have done even half of the exercises in this book, you have taken great steps toward your growth and evolution. I honor you! *[Image credit: Damedeeso@123RF.com]*

MEDITATION

Congratulations! You have made it to day 30! It only takes 21 days to establish a habit, and now the meditation can be like brushing your teeth. You wouldn't go a day without brushing your teeth or combing your hair, would you? No, it is just your habit to do these every day. Now that you are in the habit, it will be easy to keep it going. Well done you! Keep going!

THINK WITH THE HEART

Keep the light of your heart always shining. This is where true happiness comes from. This is a secret you may have discovered over this last month. The heart is precious. Nourish it, listen to it, let it speak to you and guide you. Be blessed with its wisdom and may you remember today to always keep your heart light shining brightly.

LOVE WITH THE MIND

Your mind has had a lot to digest over the last month. Let the lessons sink in. Review all your notes, and sit with the experiences you have had. On this final day set intentions for the future. Use your mind to set intentions for how you will think and act differently now that you have completed the workbook. Let love rule your life and your thoughts, and may you be so blessed!

Love and Blessings,
Paul

Notes

Resources

Meditation:

www.heartbasedmeditation.com

Healing Light Yoga:

www.healinglightyoga.com

Energetic Mastery / Intuition:

www.energeticmasterynow.com

Dr. Paul Dugliss:

www.drdugliss.com

www.pauldugliss.com

www.newworldayurveda.com